Abou

Spiritual Service

"Over a five year period, I have reached out to Mark Pope many times for help with seemingly small issues as well as with over-whelming emotional suffering. During these guidance sessions, he has always listened with compassion and empathy and gently turned my perception back to the spiritual principles he expresses in The Way of Grace. In addition, he would often suggest a book or an exercise that would give me additional insight. Since my sessions began, I have had many, many moments of grace.

"Although sometimes I still forget and spiral into a 'poor pitiful me' attitude when I strongly want events to be different, I am now able to observe this in myself much more quickly. With Mark's help, I am realizing with more clarity that my moods will come and go and that trying to change them by distraction is counterproductive. My life is definitely more peaceful and even though external circumstances do not always change, I do observe and feel them differently. I attribute my sessions with Mark as the catalyst for the changes I see in myself. I am so grateful!"

--L.R.

"Simply put, Mark Pope changed my life. I am a highly educated, professional who was born into a non-religious home. I was not given a cradle faith. In fact, I was taught that there is no place for faith -- you have to make it on your own. Mark taught me how to open up my heart center and have faith in the One Presence that is true love. He taught me to fearlessly live my life in the flow of grace. Though this book is short, it is very dense with important insights that make it worth reading many times over. When I first met Mark he told me that he was in service to help people live without suffering - to understand that we are not our thoughts and our thoughts are not the truth. He showed me how my thoughts were the result of conditioned thinking and false beliefs and that they were preventing me from living an expanded life. I have met many spiritual and religious teachers in my life but none have the insight and ability to cut to the quick as Mark does. I recommend this book and working with Mark Pope to anyone who truly wants to end suffering and live their life to the fullest."

--E. M.

"I have been receiving spiritual guidance from Mark Pope for six years. I had been in a metaphysical church for 15 years and made huge spiritual growth spurts, but the emotional pain, stress of daily life with family, and mass confusion about "my life" in general consumed my world. Mark went to great lengths to help me understand the principles he outlines in his book. I began to know the essence of my true identity—the eternal, unconditioned love of the universe. This knowing not only released emotional pain but also brought rewards in my life. Having a special needs child with emotional issues and in whose life I was intricately entwined had been painful and stressful to me for 28 years. Mark showed me how to disentangle myself from attachment to her pain and suffering so that I could better attend to her needs. And also thanks to Paul Simon's lyrics, (hop on the bus, Gus), it worked. After I no longer delved into the abyss of suffering with her, I found liberation, and so did she. Our lives have been blessed in countless ways since Mark has been diligently working with me in this teaching. My physical, emotional and financial health improved, and my daughter's quality of life has gotten overwhelmingly better (after 23 years of my asking for help, she has finally been blessed with the support of caregivers). This is only one example of how Mark's teachings have helped us. The most important one is the lesson in learning how to be present---how to disengage from thought patterns that harm us---and to just BE the awareness, the unconditional love from which we come."

--N.S.

"My appetite for understanding had me consume perhaps a hundred books on spirituality, but none addressed whatever present and particular confusion was causing my suffering. Each conversation with Mark, whether regular or infrequent, finds me precisely where I am. Mark's ability to listen, to discern, and then reveal erroneous thinking allows me to live more freely and happily. It is our one-on-one discussions that propel me forward. It's like having clarity on speed dial."

--G. F.

The Way of Grace:

An Expression of Spiritual Pointers and Principles Leading to the Wonders of Spiritual Awakening

By

Mark Pope

Table of Contents

Introduction

The purpose of this writing is to give you, the reader, a road map into a way of seeing and living that I call "the way of grace." In using the term grace, I risk the possibility that the word may mean things to you that I do not intend to convey. Still, more than 45 years after my first recognizable spiritual experience, I cannot find a better word to describe what has been revealed to me and what I have experienced time and time again. Please suspend any beliefs you may have about grace and do your best to be freshly open and receptive to what is being offered here.

My first taste of grace came in jail in 1971 while facing a life sentence. I share a few more details of that experience in Chapter Five. If you are interested in knowing more about my path, I suggest you read my autobiography, *The Final Prison Break: Adventures and Misadventures in Synchronicity, Grace and Awakening*. There I tell the more personal stories of what happened along this way of grace.

At this point it seems that the larger purpose of grace in my life is that it enables me to share the principles and pointers that may lead to this perception and/or possibility for those I serve. I was not exposed to the wonders and miracles of grace so that my ego could have its way or just to satisfy my own self-centered longings. What wisdom I have access to seems to point out that it happened in order that I might be able to clarify for others how grace can work in their lives.

Chapter One:
The Fundamental, Essential, and Absolute Truth

There is only One Presence.

The most fundamental, essential, and absolute truth is:

There is only One Presence.

Until the individual catches a glimpse, or at least deeply intuits, the truth to which these five words point, spiritual awakening by grace or by any other perceived method is not possible. Why? Because this is what we awaken into...the realization that I am and everyone is an individualized expression of this Single Presence. In fact and in truth, all forms of life, whether animate or seemingly inanimate, are expressions of this One Presence.

One of the images that may help us understand this truth is the image of an ocean over the surface of which waves arise and fall. We can say the depths of the ocean represent the infinite Source of life and the waves represent the individual forms that life takes. The ocean represents the infinite invisible Source that gives rise to these waves. The ocean then

1

represents the essential underlying reality of our most fundamental nature.

The term ocean and the image of an ocean are not the truth. They are pointing to this absolute, formless and changeless Truth. The waves, each being a temporary and yet actual expression of the ocean, are obviously not the truth either. They represent the nature of the world of form in that each wave is temporary and made up of the same essential substance as the ocean (or invisible dimension). There is no separation between the ocean and the waves. They are ONE.

Grace implies or points to the fact that there is no such thing as a separate "doer" because there is no essential or real separation. The invisible or formless dimension in which we "live, move and have our being" is the primary cause of everything. One might fairly accurately say that life is a flow of forms coming into expression, being moved and changed for a time, and then dissolving back into the Source or the Ocean. As individual expressions of the Undivided One Presence, we are being moved by the flow of Life.

During my earliest days of awakening, there arose a saying in the consciousness of many of us:

Go with the flow.

Chapter Two:
Perennial Wisdom

"In spiritual awakening, one must distinguish between simply being aware and those visible things which appear in awareness, change and eventually disappear."
–Mark Pope

In Chapter One, I introduced the ocean and waves as symbolic representations of life. It is important to understand that all images or concepts are imperfect. They can only point to what they reference. For example, the ocean represents the infinite and invisible dimension of life while a manifest ocean has limits (a bottom) and is visible. This infinite and invisible dimension is the Source of all that appears and exists. And this Presence in its invisible dimension is aware. In fact, we may rightly say it *is awareness*.

Most humans have yet to notice the distinction between awareness and the objects that appear in awareness. Awareness is overlooked in favor of an often obsessive interest and concern with the objects which appear in (and disappear from) awareness.

By "objects in awareness," I mean all things which move and change. Some examples include people, physical bodies (which are born, undergo many changes and then die and dissolve), places, possessions, careers, relationships, seasons of the year, and the weather. Other examples of somewhat subtle and/or less visible objects in awareness include physical sensations, emotions, thoughts, moods, and beliefs. All of these come, are subject to change, and go. What does not change is the awareness in which they appear.

One definition of perennial is: "continuing without interruption." This is the case with pure and simple awareness. Once again, we may rightly say, in relation to our ocean and wave analogy, that the ocean *is awareness*. On the other hand, the objects (waves) which move through awareness are in a constant state of flux. What I am referring to as perennial wisdom is seeing this distinction between what is always coming, going, moving, or changing, and that which is timeless or eternal within us. This timeless and eternal dimension of being is who we are in essence. Having overlooked or forgotten our own essential being, we become entranced by and obsessed with the "things of the world."

See if you can simply rest in and as simple awareness. Let go of any concern for the objects which are moving through awareness. Detach from them. Let them be. In so doing, you will be practicing true meditation; which simply means resting as awareness. When we rest from our concern with those things which "come and go" in awareness and when we return attention to the very Source of our existence, we begin to awaken from the trance-like spell of spiritual sleep. In scripture we find the following:

Return unto me and I will return unto thee.(Zech. 1:3)

This is a spiritual call and promise. The "me" and the "I" are not meant literally. The words are simply suggesting that there is a subtle magnetic drawing of our attention back to the Source of our existence. When we notice this internal calling and follow it by allowing our attention to return to and rest in its Source (simple awareness), we find that the nature of this Source reveals itself to us.

And so, by grace, not by doing more or by doing anything but by simply resting in and as awareness, we begin to awaken from being lost in concern for *things*. And the wonders of unconditional love, inspiration, wisdom, and other invisible characteristics of our essential nature (the ocean) begin to reveal themselves to us.

Scripture says, "seek first the kingdom and all these things shall be added unto thee." When we rest or let go of our concern for the manifest, life begins to support us and sustain us in ways that appear wondrous or even miraculous. The "Way of Grace" becomes more evident to us.

Chapter Three
Conditioned Consciousness

"The human condition: lost in thought"
–Eckhart Tolle

Each of us is in essence unconditioned. Our deepest nature is ocean-like in that it is formless and invisible consciousness/awareness. When we are born into a body, we immediately begin to undergo the process of conditioning. We are taught by perhaps well-meaning but spiritually asleep authority figures to believe that who we are is this body. And we are taught to identify ourselves as a male or female, a member of a nation, and on and on. We learn pretty quickly that certain behaviors are rewarded and others punished. And we begin to adopt and build a personality (from **persona**, meaning mask).

We also adopt a set of values from the information to which we are exposed. We begin to believe that *who we are* is this body and this personality (mask). Please note the very term *information* suggests this is all in the world of "form." Consciousness gets lost in and identifies with all this in-form-ation.

Meanwhile, our deepest and eternal nature begins to be forgotten and lost from view. We begin to believe our thoughts without much, if any, ability to discern the difference between awareness and the thoughts and beliefs that appear in awareness. Most of us no longer even notice the vast (actually infinite) and unconditioned dimension of our own being.

Through this conditioning, we lose sight of the very Source of our existence. We begin to be obsessively concerned with what we perceive in the world of form. The formless dimension, for the majority of us, ceases to hold any significance. Even the so-called search for God is often seen as a search for the right information or the right belief system or the right guru, or the right practice. So we are thereby temporarily consigned to a vain and futile search for the infinite invisible Source of our existence where, of course, it cannot be found...in the world of forms and beliefs.

And this search, if we are predisposed to go on a spiritual search at all, is usually motivated by a false premise. The false premise is we actually believe that who we are is a little separate body and personality (again, from **persona**, meaning mask). If one looks closely at what is being pointed at here, we see that the fundamental basis of our spiritual search is that we believe we are separate from that which we seek and are thereby driven to search for our own innermost being "out there" somewhere in the world of form. We are looking for our own sacred nature, the very Source of our existence where it can never be found because we have overlooked the fact of our own infinite and formless nature which is pure and simple unconditioned awareness.

This is what the quote from Eckhart Tolle above is suggesting. We are lost in thought. And our search is often taking place in a world of thoughts and beliefs that fail to even mention this primary and unconditioned dimension of our being.

Chapter Four
Unconditional Love

In real love, you want the other person's good. In romantic love you want the other person.

–Margaret Anderson

Our unconditioned nature or essence is not simply unconditioned awareness. It is also unconditioned/ unconditional love. When we see the world through the eyes of our unconditioned essence, what we see is the Single Presence expressing itself in, through and as all that we see. We see this **as it is** and not through a set of conditioned and self-centered beliefs.

This unconditioned love is infinitely deep and wise. Without needing to "think" about it, it is evident that the One Presence expressing as another person is as spiritually awake as is possible for them to be at that moment. We may recognize that another person is caught in their conditioning and we understand that with a kind of mercy and compassion that are natural to who we are.

We do not see them as existing to meet our needs, or to hurt us. We just understand. And we cannot help but feel a sense of compassion since we know from experience what it is like to be trapped in the limited perspective this entails.

Romantic love is a kind of egoic delusion in which we imagine that another person will or can meet the needs of our "little needy" (false or conditioned) self. We project this impossible task on the other. And eventually we are destined to be disappointed.

We are not here to get. We are an individualization of the infinite potential to give and to love. We are infinite and unconditioned love and awareness temporarily and uniquely embodied. Our purpose is to awaken to this, after which we naturally understand and appreciate others exactly as they are. A paradox comes into play here. When we see others through the eyes of love instead of wanting something, we automatically respond in ways that are most helpful to them. We also feel a sense of wholeness and a gratitude for the ability and opportunity to be of essential value to those we encounter.

There is a saying in scripture that may seem strange on the face of it:

"To the one that hath, even more shall be given, while to the one that hath not, even that which they hath shall be taken." (Matt. 25:29)

The quote points out that when we are lost in identification with a conditioned and needy sense of self (believing we lack what we need), we will experience losses as deeply personal and emotionally painful. When we awaken to who we are (expressions of infinite potential), we begin to experience life as a flow of grace whereby things, often wondrously, fall into place, and by which we experience a sense of fulfillment.

You are already the "one that hath." Spiritual awakening is awakening from the dream of being a "little needy" person separate from everyone and everything. It is awakening to who you already are and always have been. That is the value of the analogy. It is pointing to our potential to simply awaken from a dream. The fact that most humans are still asleep and dreaming is what causes the dream to seem so real.

Rest in and as your unconditioned nature. Cease believing every thought that arises. See even the conditioned thoughts through the eyes of love and understanding. Being born on earth is pretty much a guarantee that you have undergone the process of conditioning and have been temporarily lost in the dream.

Who you are as unconditioned awareness and love is not really lost, and you have never been separated by it. It has only been overlooked. Most of us have fallen into a spell that our beliefs have cast.

Break the spell. Cease believing the rather continuous stream of conditioned thoughts. Awaken by seeing life as it actually is in the here and now, without labels and judgments. See with the eyes of your truest, deepest self. See with the eyes of True Love.

Chapter Five
The Heart Center as Portal into Grace

"The awakening of the Heart Center is the acme of spiritual development."
–Brugh Joy

Of all the spiritual resources I have encountered and experienced, one stands out as the most significant. That one is the awakening of the heart center.

There are seven primary spiritual centers (chakras) built into the body. Each one, when activated or awakened, gives rise to specific resources and perceptions. The heart center is located in the center of these seven with three above and three below. It is symbolized in some Buddhist and Hindu traditions by a circle with lotus petals around it and with a six-pointed star (two equal triangles joined) within the circle. This image suggests the union of the six other centers.

Most everyone has seen the image of Jesus with a kind of fiery heart in the middle of the chest. Often such images also depict Jesus pointing to this center. Some call it the sacred heart. Others have named this center of consciousness the love center. When awakened or activated, this center causes indescribable love to enter awareness. This love, which I will term **divine love**, is unlike any of our conditioned ideas of love. It is indeed like a fire that consumes everything false. Previous limited beliefs and concepts about love are transmuted into the actual experience of a love to which all things are instantly made possible. One knows in such a moment of awakening that one has encountered a power that comes from beyond our limited sense of self. And quite significantly, we experience such an awakening, not as something unfamiliar, but as something valuable beyond measure that had been forgotten or lost from view.

Nothing we will ever know or experience can be of greater value than this awakening. It is an experience or direct encounter with unconditional love. And this love is transforming. It changes us forever, often in less than the blink of an eye.

This "divine love" is the very essence of what I mean when I refer to grace.

In the moment one is touched by it, one knows beyond doubt that it does not come through having earned it, or deserved it, or caused it to arise into awareness. This "divine love" allows one entry into the land of what our conditioned mind calls the miraculous.

This little book of teachings is meant to be largely impersonal. However, in order to give this set of pointers to the amazing resources of the heart center its appropriate emphasis, I will give a brief personal testimonial here.

"In 1971, after having spent some seven years incarcerated in jails, prisons, and other institutions, I found myself in jail again under a $300,000 bond and facing a life sentence for crimes I did not commit. At the same time, some rather convincing circumstantial evidence suggested I was guilty. Several months into my time in jail, I underwent an experience whereby this "divine love" flooded my awareness and altered me forever. Fear was dissolved and turned into love. I was introduced to a power beyond my wildest imaginings. My circumstance was also altered in dramatic, one might even say miraculous, fashion. A few weeks later, all charges were dismissed based on a legal technicality. I was freed and never locked up again. A perceived lifetime of difficulties and victimhood was transformed into a life of spiritual interest and service." –Mark Pope

This "divine love" is the very essence of who we are. It lies largely dormant and forgotten in most of us. Perhaps we catch a fleeting glimpse of it from time to time. This power that can change us forever and at great depth is always already shining in us and is our deepest and truest self.

Although we cannot *cause* this center to awaken, it does so in its own time, often in degrees, when we give our attention to it. Simply touching the center of the chest and inviting this grace to emerge and reveal itself is helpful. There is an ancient principle which has been stated as follows:

We experience that to which we give our attention.

Most of us have given the majority of our attention to the things of the world...to the things that appear in awareness. We have innocently forgotten our spiritual inheritance. Like prodigal children, we often have to suffer great losses before we become willing to re-evaluate our priorities. Still, the spiritual call, the subtle magnetic pull to return our attention to the Source of our being, continues forever. It is the call to return to our truest nature which is an unselfish love that literally radiates from our core. It is a call to a love that can change us at depth forever...a love that will destroy our false beliefs and our erroneous perceptions...a love that reveals the interrelatedness of all things to all things...a love that forgives the seemingly unforgivable. As the Andrew Lloyd Webber lyrics proclaim, *"love changes everything."*

The reason we cannot *earn*, *deserve* or *cause* grace is because it is already given, and already caused, and already present. This grace is what is always calling us from the very center of our being, saying, as it were...

"Return unto me and I will return unto thee."

Chapter 6
Being the Witness

"What happens is, consciousness disentangles itself from identification with the conditioned sense of self."
–Eckhart Tolle

Let us return to the distinction between awareness and "objects" in awareness. The ability to see this distinction for oneself is, for most of us, essential to awakening from identification with our conditioning.

We are not our thoughts. And the vast majority of the thoughts that arise into awareness (here I am speaking about the self-concerned thoughts that typically begin with "I" or reference "me") are simply this conditioning masquerading as a separate self. It is really a simple matter to notice that thoughts come and go while our unfettered awareness is always present and is witnessing this activity.

The practice of witnessing thoughts is of enormous value in the process of awakening. As long as the voice in the head can say "I" or "me," and we somehow believe that this voice actually is who we are, we will remain trapped in a conceptual prison of psychological conditioning. And we remain identified with this conditioned and ultimately false sense of self. It is very much like being under a spell or in a trance, which is why it is commonly referred to as a dream from which one may "awaken."

Conversely, once we realize that we can witness these thoughts, we are beginning to awaken to who we are. We are breaking the spell. When we are able to simply watch thoughts come and go, we are doing so from pure unconditioned awareness. And this awareness is our essential being.

A number of years ago, I was in Malibu, California as part of a studio audience during the filming of a session of Eckhart Tolle TV. I was sitting in the front row while Eckhart was making this point. We had a brief interaction whereby he pointed out what happens when we are able to witness these conditioned thoughts without needing to believe them or identify them as "my thoughts." He said:

"What happens is, consciousness disentangles itself from identification with our conditioned sense of self."

In my experience, Eckhart tends away from drama and instead makes simple statements that can lead to liberation. Freedom from being trapped within swirl-ing, repetitive, self-centered thoughts and concerns is of the essence. And it depends upon our ability to witness our thoughts.

This very idea can seem preposterous to those who are completely identified with what Eckhart calls the "story of me." This is partly because nearly everyone is living in their story, and it has not yet occurred to them that there is a sense of being that is deeper than thought. And it certainly doesn't occur to most people that this dimension of being is already free of all psychological suffering.

Most human beings are in fact utterly lost in thought.

Are you able to sit still and witness the thoughts that come and go? Can you see that they are mostly useless and repetitive chatter? Can you see how believing they are of utmost importance or believing them to be true causes you to suffer?

Can you see that who you are cannot be thoughts because they come and go? Perhaps it is evident to you that your most essential self cannot be found in thoughts. What is it that is always here? Is it not the background field of awareness in which these thoughts and things are registering? Without awareness, you would not know a thought was occurring...or that it was dissolving.

Awareness is the eternal essence of who you are. Notice awareness never resists what appears within it. It is somewhat like a mirror in that it simply reflects what appears in it. Awareness makes no comments or judgments. Awareness has no opinions. It simply watches what comes and goes. Awareness is innocent and sees all that arises through the eyes of innocence. When we remember who we are as pure unconditioned awareness, we are no longer imprisoned within a world of conditioned beliefs. And we can see that even if others are still imprisoned, they are not what they believe either. They too are innocent. They are just temporarily trapped in the same prison in which we were once trapped. Awareness is not simply seeing. It is pure unconditioned wisdom and love. When we reawaken to this, we become a redeeming and healing presence in the world, not by what we say or do, but because we are free from the distorted perceptions of ego.

Sarah McLachlan sings a song entitled "Adia" that seems to be to a former lover. The lyrics seem to partially convey, poetically, what I am saying to you now:

> *There's no one left to finger*
> *There's no one here to blame*
> *…And there ain't no one to buy our innocence*
> *'Cause we are born innocent*
> *(And) we are still innocent*
> *It's easy, we all falter,*
> *Does it matter?*

Chapter Seven
Emotional Pain

"Resistance creates persistence"--unknown

"We heal (free painful emotional energy) by holding it in a field of unconditional love and compassion. At essence, you are that love and compassion."
–Mark Pope

Emotional pain is held in place by false beliefs. Sometimes these beliefs are not immediately known to our surface mind. This pain arises into awareness and is usually accompanied by thoughts that will tend to keep it in place if we believe them. Examples of the type of thoughts that arise when we are experiencing such pain are, "Something is wrong with me," or "I am not good enough," or "I shouldn't be feeling this," or "somebody caused this pain."

In actuality, emotional pain has been trapped within us by these kinds of thoughts and is arising in order to provide us with an opportunity to release or liberate the pain from its conceptual entrapment.

The surface mind cannot free us from emotional pain. Its thoughts or beliefs are usually tactics or strategies that mislead us.

What liberates the emotional pain and permits it to dissipate is the simple practice of **allowing it to be** and seeing it from the heart, or with compassion. By simply witnessing it without believing any thoughts, judgments or opinions allows the pain to move through awareness without resistance. And resisting the pain, mentally pushing and pulling on it, will only cause it to persist. One might also say that allowing it to be there and witnessing it with compassion will cause it to dissolve and free it from the prison of false beliefs.

It is natural, given the conditioning we undergo, to believe there is something wrong when we are hurting and want to do something to get rid of the pain, but it just doesn't really help. What helps is unconditional acceptance (love). The strategies of the conditioned mind may seem to make logical sense, but they cannot help us get to the root cause.

The root cause is a false belief. If we can just sit still and watch the pain with even a little compassion, we will be able to see the kinds of thoughts or beliefs that have this painful energy trapped in us. And then we can see with understanding what caused us to have such pain in us to start with. We can then choose not to identify with these thoughts.

Emotional pain is trapped in almost all of us. If we believe pain is being caused by outer circumstances, no matter the evidence that may seem to support such a conclusion, we can never fully escape it. If we believe there is something inherently wrong with us, we cannot escape it. Yes, it may become latent, but it will always return until we see the cause and disentangle ourselves from identification with the belief. We must get to the root. And the root is always believing something that is untrue.

Anything we believe that suggests the pain should not be there is false. It IS there. Anything we do to resist the pain only strengthens it and leaves it in place with the potential to rise again and again. The world we live in is a world of people who mostly believe resistance is the way to deal with anything unpleasant. The world is mistaken and confused.

"Resistance creates persistence."

"We heal (free painful emotional energy) by holding it in a field of unconditional love and compassion. At essence, you are that love and compassion."

Emotional pain and its causes have been passed down to us for generations through the conditioning we receive beginning at a very young age. We absorb this conditioning, perhaps a bit like osmosis. The fact that we have it is no one's fault. It can be attributed to the fact that we were born onto a planet of mostly unconscious and perhaps spiritually asleep human beings who were, nonetheless, doing the best they could, given their conditioning.

Looking for the cause in our earlier life or in circumstances just keeps us looking in the wrong direction. To paraphrase the lyrics from Sarah McLachlan's song again,

"You were born innocent and you are innocent still."

Fortunately, the subtle power of pure unconditioned awareness, divine love, and compassion **are in you now and forever**. They are your true nature. The conditioned sense of self with its false beliefs and its emotional pain are **not** who you are. And yet these difficulties will plague us until we either are driven or choose to return our attention to who we are. Resting and witnessing emotional pain with mercy and awareness—resting and observing the imprisoning beliefs that have kept this pain trapped in us—allows it to pass.

You are not the cause of your emotional pain. You did not consciously choose to believe things that would create or cause pain. And yet, only you can free yourself from it. And paradoxically, there is nothing you need to do. Just rest as a compassionate witness and do not get lost in or believe the thoughts that accompany the pain, and it will dissolve.

Chapter Eight
Autonomy and the Unlived Life

Just get on the bus, Gus,
You don't need to discuss much,
Just drop off the key, Lee
And get yourself free
–"50 ways to leave your lover" by Paul Simon

Cultural values can have an enormous influence on the individual. The reason for this goes largely unnoticed. The conditioned sense of self is derived out of fear. And our culture is fear-based. This fear is not always immediately evident. This fear-based value system which is unconsciously accepted by the majority of humans is what Jesus refers to when he uses the term "the world."

One must eventually question this system. And to question it is a radical departure from the group or the collective. In scripture, Jesus offers the parable of the one sheep in a flock of 100 who leaves the 99 and heads off alone. Then we are told the shepherd goes in search of the one and rejoices upon finding it.

This may appear nonsensical to the unawakened. A strictly linear or rational interpretation is useless. What is suggested is precisely what I am saying above. One must step away from the group-think of the collective. One must be willing to step away from the influence of the majority and look beyond this sleep-inducing, imprisoning perspective. There is a way of living that cannot be perceived when we are trapped in the fear-based value system of the world.

For example, I imagine that most of those who read these words have already undergone some of the difficulties that can occur when we step away from the popularly held opinions of the world. Many of us have rejected the fundamental religious beliefs of our families or friends. We may have been warned that our souls are in danger of "going to hell."

However, the symbol of the shepherd represents Life or the greater spiritual reality. The declaration of a greater love for the one who risks this radical departure from the group means that once we find the courage or adventurousness to take this risk, it translates into being open to a grace that otherwise may not have been realized.

A life that otherwise could not have been imagined begins to open and unfold for us. No longer trapped in a fear-based system, we find that the previously UN-lived possibilities and potentials within us begin to emerge and be realized.

Autonomy means living from our own internal sense of integrity. It means we take risks and are willing to accept the results simply because it seems better than taking someone else's word for it.

We cannot remain in the conceptual prison of the majority and be free. In quoting the lyrics of Paul Simon's song, I'm not advocating leaving someone you love. They are hinting at how we are imprisoned by fear and the attachments fear engenders. I am using these lyrics to remind you that you may be trapped in fear. We cannot hold on in fear and let go into freedom. I am reminding you that freedom from fear is yours to claim and is precious. That is why it is often referred to as liberation!!!

Here are the opening lyrics to the song:

The problem is all inside your head she said to me
The answer is easy if you take it logically
I'd like to help you in your struggle to be free
There must be fifty ways to leave your lover (or your attachments)

She said it's really not my habit to intrude
Furthermore, I hope my meaning won't be lost or misconstrued
But I'll repeat myself at the risk of being crude
There must be fifty ways to leave your lover
Fifty ways to leave your lover

Chapter Nine
Non-Resistance & Miracles and Wonders

"To offer no resistance to life is to be in a state of grace, ease, and lightness."
–unknown

"Resistance is futile."
–Star Trek

Reality is **what is** in this moment. Period. I do not speak of consensual reality or other people's reality but only of what is for you, now, in this moment. Suchness is another term that points out what is.

The conditioned mind is a resistance machine that operates in us, often with great momentum. Can you step back, so to speak, and see the barrage of commentary arising from the conditioned mind? Try seeing it with compassion and mercy. Notice how much of what it says is in opposition to what is in this holy instant. If you can see it, there will no longer be any mystery to why human beings suffer so much.

As normal as it is to argue with or oppose what is, it is also insane. And it is an exercise in futility. Perhaps you recall the words uttered in a Star Trek episode many years ago:

"Resistance is futile."

Resisting **what is** in the present moment is the cause of all psychological suffering. The conditioned mind may tell us it is hard to keep from getting caught in this conditioned thinking. This is false. It is much harder to remain trapped in its insane machinations.

What can we do about this? How about simply viewing these conditioned, resistant, and oppositional thoughts with mercy and compassion? If conditioned thoughts that resist reality are arising, then **that is what is**. Strictly speaking, ego is resistance to what is. And to resist the resistant thoughts is one of ego's favorite ploys. It is as if the ego divides itself into two sides and one side attacks the other.

The only solution is to witness this dysfunctional and resistant thinking with compassion and mercy. You did not consciously choose to create this conditioning. It just happened at a time when neither you nor anyone around you knew any better.

It is only in identifying these thoughts as "mine," or in believing these thoughts that we suffer. When we witness or observe them with compassion, our essential self or being disentangles itself from this mistaken sense of self, and the emotional energy trapped in these "resistant" concepts is released.

Freedom from egoic traps can only be found now—in this moment. When, in this moment, we see our conditioned and resistant thoughts with mercy and compassion, miracles and wonders occur. Suddenly, we are free from the traps. This experience has been called a holy instant. We cannot achieve or earn it. It is not a *doing*. It is simply a seeing with love and understanding.

The patterns in which most humans are trapped create and recreate circumstances and emotional reactions that then create and recreate themselves again and again. This is what is meant by karma, or the karmic wheel. We cannot find freedom by fighting against these patterns. Freedom happens when we stop fighting and let life be as it is...and by simply seeing and accepting **what is as it is**.

Here is a great paradox and a miracle. Once we stop fighting...and let life be as it is...even let the conditioned mind be there as it is...the patterns are weakened and begin to dissolve. Life becomes miraculously more benign.

There is no future time in which this can happen. It can only happen now. ***This is the Holy Instant***. Now. Cease identifying with the conditioned mind and it will instantly begin to lose strength.

This is the portal into the miraculous and the wondrous. And I do not mean miraculous and wondrous things begin to occur, though that is likely, too. I am saying that the burden of ego begins to drop away. Resistance requires enormous energy and is a burden and a drain. Once we let go, unexpected grace appears. An ease and lightness that was always already there appears.

"Let go and let God" is a common mantra in many spiritual teachings. It does not mean do nothing. It means doing without attachment to outcome. It is pointing to the possibility of being free from identifying with burdensome, conditioned, and resistant thoughts that keep us on the wheel of suffering.

Many people believe that unless we resist things they will never change. And that is true from the ego's tiny perspective. There is another way...an easier way...a way filled with miracles and wonders...a way where self-concern and fear are no longer the driving motives of our existence.

It may not make sense to the conditioned mind. It may not make sense to your friends or family. But deep in your heart you know it is the only way to ever really be free. It is the way of acceptance of what is. It is the way of non-resistance. It is the way of grace.

Let go of the illusion of personal power and control. Let go and let God reveal the truly miraculous and wondrous. At this point...in this holy instant...the deepest truth is revealed as grace upon grace upon grace.

"To offer no resistance to life is to be in a state of grace, ease, and lightness."

Chapter 10
Attention and Pointers

"The analysis of pointers is pointless."
–Eckhart Tolle

All spiritual teaching can do is point to the Truth of your being. The Truth is not a concept. Infinite and formless Love, Wisdom, and Presence are your essential being. This little book is intended to simply provide some pointers for you. That is to say, it is intended to point your attention toward your essence...to point or guide you out of being lost in thinking.

Many people seem incapable of distinguishing between their thoughts and attention. Attention can be directed to thoughts or to something other than thoughts. For example, at this moment, you can give your attention to your right foot or to your heart center. In either case you will notice that neither your right foot nor your heart center are thinking.

All spiritual teaching can do is help guide you out of the conceptual prison of conditioned consciousness in which most humans live.

I used many pointers that were provided by spiritual teachers along the way. Some were more helpful than others. I will conclude this writing by sharing some of my favorite pointers. May they guide you back into the wonders and grace of your true nature. May they point the way into liberation from the confines of ego and into the land of miracles and wonders.

"Here is a new spiritual practice for you: Don't take your thoughts too seriously."
–Eckhart Tolle

"When we stop opposing reality, action becomes simple, fluid, kind, and fearless."
–Eckhart Tolle

"All delusions begin in the mind. All delusions are based on various ways we're talking to ourselves and then believing what we are saying."
–Adyashanti

"When you argue with reality, you lose, but only 100% of the time."
–Byron Katie

"You can be right or you can be free. Which do you want?"
–Byron Katie

"Identify your painful thought, question it and wake yourself up. No one else can."
–Adyashanti

"When you think everything is someone else's fault, you will suffer a lot. When you think everything is your fault, you will also suffer a lot."
–Byron Katie

"Worry pretends to be necessary but serves no useful purpose."
–unknown

"What a liberation to realize that the "voice in my head" is not who I am. Who am I then? The one who sees that."
–Eckart Tolle

"When you don't cover up the world with words and labels, a sense of the miraculous returns to your life that was lost a long time ago when humanity, instead of using thought, became possessed by thought."
–Eckhart Tolle

"Words reduce reality to something the human mind can grasp, which isn't very much."
–Adyashanti

"All negative reactions are wake up calls reminding us that we are believing our thoughts. Question your thoughts and wake yourself up from the dream. Or not."

–Adyashanti

"Life is simple. Everything happens for you, not to you. Everything happens at exactly the right moment, neither too soon nor too late. You don't have to like it... it's just easier if you do."

–Byron Katie

"Enlightenment is nothing more than the complete absence of resistance to what is. End of story."

–Adyashanti

Afterword

I provide personal services in the form of specific guidance into living in the Way of Grace to those who may be inclined to ask. You may contact me by email at markjacksonpope@gmail.com. These services are provided on a donation basis. Suggested minimum donation is $75 per hour.

A Wave of Grace,

Mark Pope

51544133R00028

Made in the USA
Columbia, SC
19 February 2019